IN THE SHADOW OF PARADISE

JANE ELLEN GLASSER

FUTURECYCLE PRESS

www.futurecycle.org

Library of Congress Control Number: 2016963605

Published by FutureCycle Press
Lexington, Kentucky, USA

ISBN 978-1-942371-29-8

In memory of my beloved mother,
who nurtured my imagination.

CONTENTS

I

II

III

IV

V

Acknowledgments

The imperfect is our paradise.
—Wallace Stevens

The wound is the place where the light enters you.
—Rumi

I

Rousseau's Last Painting

This could be Eden, a realm of exotic,
lush vegetation, but the tree of knowledge
is missing, the snake that tempted Eve
slithers from the canvas, and a black man,
his loins brightly masked, replaces Adam.

This could be Paradise, its fruit forever
unspoiled on the orange tree, wild beasts
peacefully commingling, hypertrophic
lotuses perfuming the air, the enchantment
of birdsong and a flute's silvery sighs.

This could be a dream, the imagination's
longing for the impossible: a classical nude
on a red divan transported to a primeval
jungle. A lion's wide-eyed gaze invites you in.
You are the viewer. You are the dreamer.

Daphne's Plea

Help me, Father! Open the earth
to enclose me, or change my form.

I refuse to trade my woodlands
for the tomb of a marriage house.

Don't speak to me of grandchildren!

Bobolinks sing lullabies sweeter than I
who would rather romp barefoot
with the rabbit and the red fox

than be cracked open like a mollusk
to let Apollo in. These hips
were not meant to dandle babies.

Keep me safe, Father,
from the hard wants of a man.

If I must be rooted, plant my feet
in rich soil, let my womanly flesh
harden to bark, and let my limbs,

robust in sleeves of evergreen,
keep reaching for the sun.

What She Longed For

To slip out of her past
the way an unzipped dress
puddles to the floor;

to empty the mind
and feel it flap
like a windsock;

to let spirit play,
dust motes
on ladders of light;

to set her senses
singing
through all her organs;

to dance
across continents
while standing still.

CRACKS

If you look closely,
Mona Lisa's lips
are chapped
with cracks.

In Rilke's elegy
death zigzags
on a china cup.

Don't give me
perfection
immune to clocks.

Don't give me
the unbroken,
the safely stored
in airless vaults.

Every scar
is the shorthand
of an important story.

Each crack
is a door opening
onto a larger room.

David, O David

The strain of holding a classic pose,
one leg supporting your great weight
for five hundred years, no wonder
in pre-pubescent youth you're old.

Fractures, weak ankles, the contrapposto
of hips and shoulders torqued
in opposing angles—an earthquake,
or simply construction in the streets

of Florence could topple you. Though
the curve of your torso sets stillness
in motion, you stand stalled between
decision and action, between what is

and what is to come. Is that Goliath
approaching who has turned your head,
brow drawn and neck tensed for the
contest that will glorify your name?

David, O David, isn't this the stance
of humankind—unbalanced, quotidian
lives battling the giant of Time—
waiting for their crowning moment?

THE RUNAWAY

After *Freedom—The Carousel* by Anne Wipf

For fifty years, my forelegs arced
in air, mane and tail flying,
round and round, up and down
I galloped to circus music,

the happiest sounds on Earth.
I told myself I was content.
Wasn't it enough to be part of a
rotating world of children's smiles?

Bound by habit, I stuck to my post,
circling a cramped corral, ridden
but always denied the ride.
In night's stall, abandoned,

I dreamed of wind raking my back,
my hooves stamping U-U-U
across grassy fields, free
to say neigh to the life

carved out for me. What value
has a life that keeps going
and goes nowhere? I threw off
the heavy saddle, the bridle, the reins.

I left a trail for the children.

Paradise on the Patio

Early morning, the bird
of paradise's giant
fronds rustle,

soothing as waves
receding
on a foam-tatted shore.

Overhead,
the sun winks through
the ragged canopy

as clouds
touch and separate
like one-night lovers.

Such bliss
is an evening primrose
that fades at dawn.

Doused in light
these white blooms
born wingless

through narrow sheaths
are content,
as I am now

in the shadow
of Paradise,
to stay fixed.

Day's End

Such release, the sky paling, the backlit clouds
melting on the horizon. It feels good to fade
at day's end, to be happily empty—a simple bowl
set in one place, free of the weight of apples,
pears, grapes. Though some deliciousness
remains. At lunch today I sat beside a friend,
savoring her closeness while I only played
with a serving of lobster bisque. Now the sky
is a hundred shades of grey and street lights
come on. Outside my window the fronds
of a foxtail appear to enjoy a slow dance
with the wind. All night they will dance.
I kissed a woman today. So different from
kissing a man. Such release, the soft darkness
that touches and connects everything.

How to Ripen

Picked green, sour, odorless, hard,

place Bartlett pears
in a brown paper bag, seal tight;

submerge mangoes
in a copious container of rice;

infiltrate one ripe kiwifruit
in a bowl of green plums;

like a Cézanne painting, lay peaches
on a clean linen towel, cover with another;

let a banana and avocado on the counter
quicken with touch;

in a straw basket, watch passion
fruit make love to honeydew.

Oh, what propinquity and
climacteric hormones produce!

ONE APPLE

Why claim the whole orchard
or even one tree bowed
with fruit, at its base
a devil of bees feasting?

One is enough for a treatise
on beauty, sin, and death.
What else could tell us
so much about ourselves,

we who were schooled by Eve,
a queen pandering poison,
the worm. Just one granted
access to the Elysian Fields,
slammed Eden's Gates.

Cézanne swore he'd astonish
Paris with an apple, and he did.

THE MANDATE

Fifty years locked away in La Casa Azul,
the place where Frida Kahlo was born,
the place where Frida Kahlo died,
her personal possessions:

common as a toothbrush, a compact,
ribbons, cat-eye sunglasses,
used-up bottles of Revlon nail polish;

uncommon as a prosthetic leg,
its red boot belled, body casts painted
from a mirror above her bed;

the Tehuana skirts and blouses,
increasingly adorned
with lace and embroidery
to keep measure with the intricate
stitchery of pain.

Who can explain the actions of men!

No record exists of Rivera's motive
to seal away in the bathroom
the personal belongings of a wife

who would die before him,
who would outlive him.

THE SEAFARER'S WIFE

After She Sees Things Differently by Heather Watts

Time has anchored her to this strand of beach.

Flies hum above clumped seaweed.
Stars are strewn at her feet.

On a rocky promontory
a lighthouse blinks story after story
of rescued hope and shipwrecked faith.

Her eyes roll up, twin moons
in the heaven of her face

as again she carries him home.

THE SIREN AND THE POET

After Marc Chagall

Resting his head against the flames of the
Siren's tresses, the poet is beside himself.
Who better to instruct him on the art of voice,
so enchanting sailors could not resist?

A mermaid's tail replaces the wings of myth.
Pearls grace her neck. The poet's embrace
lifts her from the ocean as if he must pull
from his own depths the music of longing.

So like this Muse of the Lower World,
the poet sets sail across time's turbulent seas
to discover, in *spiritus,* the right music and
words to connect beauty, love, and death.

Ars Poetica

A poem about sipping tea
in a late afternoon drowse
might take the shape
of a steaming kettle.

While meter and rhyme
fitted to form
traditionally tame the mess
of love and loss,

modernists let
the beast break out,
ecstatic in the land
of Anything-Goes.

The possibilities are infinite
when playing god.

ADRIFT

How many times have you been adrift—
a small craft caught between the cataract
eye of the moon in a cloud-suffused sky
and the white-lipped ocean, far from sure
ground? No paddles. No motor. No wind-
billowed sails to ride the swells home.

This happens, you know, even on land
when you stand, awash in sunlight,
a body in the company of other bodies,
relinquishing your soul to the
slap-slap-slap of waves on a hull.

Freight of Moods

At the mercy
of moon and wind,
Doldrums dip
to Lethe's depths.
Anchored in muck
my days stall
in Listlessness.

Black clouds amass.
Aeolus whips up
squalls, perilously
rocking the ship.
Fear clings to Hope
as if screams
could pacify an ocean.

No maps, no compass,
no guiding stars,
the prow plowing
an aimless course,
I'm Lost, Desperate,
an infinitesimal dot
rimmed by flat horizons.

Across a lapping,
moonlit main,
the Sirens' strains
beckon me.

Who but Odysseus
could resist
drowning in Bliss?

A new dawn,
Zephyr calming
sun-spattered waves
steers Contentment
safely to shore.

Bored, Restless
as salts on liberty, again
my moods set sail
for unknown ports.

The Politics of Fingers

Thumb

Who is more important than I?
Emperor of the will,
top man in a fist, I am able
to hold the others in place.
Thumbs up/thumbs down—
I authorize or condemn.
Children love me;
a surrogate tit, I silence cries
and comfort distress.

Forefinger

Who is the thumb kidding?
One phalange short, he needs
my connection to OK
anything. Crooked and waving,
I beckon. Straight and wagging,
I tame impudence. Aka
pointer, Uncle Sam's summons,
I single out for punishment or glory.
Who can say I am not No. 1,
the trigger finger, the victory sign!

Middle Finger

Digitus impudicus, I am shameless.
A one-finger salute, the flashed
bird of contempt, I am the favorite
of pissed-off drivers, politicians,

movie stars, hooligans. A symbolic
phallus, I make all important decisions.
What other finger has earned
a thirty-six foot statue, giving the finger
to the stock exchange in Milan!*

Ring Finger

Don't the others know only love
can drive out hate! *Vena amoris,*
ruler of the heart, what is more
honorable than a kept commitment?
How many times I have tried
to save the world through love.
Alas! Easy as flicking a switch,
my crown goes on, comes off.

Pinkie

They call me names: baby, runt,
tag along. They say I am affected,
daintily raised for sipping tea.
What do they know of manners!
Teamed they become barbaric,
disparaging utensils. Linked
with another's pinkie, I alone
swear to keep agreements. Once,
a broken promise meant amputation.
Let them try living without me!

*Sculpture by Maurizio Cattelan

Two Crows

Two crows lay on a bed of needles,
heads wrenched sideways,
wings splayed like broken fans.

I could read it as an omen,
one crow hurled from a great height,
but knowing, as gods do,
human resistance to dark signs,
a second plummeted to the ground.

I could call it a battlefield,
violence born of hubris or revenge
that ends with the heart bursting
its million feathers.

I could stage it as a tragedy,
the beloved shot from the sky,
the other, gutted by grief,
who sacrificed his life.

I could bury the crows in my yard,
but then my cat, or something cat-like,
would surely paw the dirt
to place an offering at my feet.

A Sign from Above

In memory of my daughter, Jessica

Rudderless, windswept,
a Goodyear blimp
sails the skies.

Is anyone home steering
the great airship?

Clockmaker theorists
would argue
an abandoned design.

As a child
on my knees at night
I was taught to pray.
I believed *Elohim*
had ears and a heart
like my father.

In slow, relentless circles
the blimp repeats
and repeats itself.

Centuries ago,
mankind imagined
the angel-filled heavens
as an ocean with ports
offering safe passage.

I think of my daughter
driving home from college
while God slept.

WHEN HIS BROTHER DIED

When his brother died
a silent scream—
like wind-ripped leaves—
swirled to an island
across the sea.

When his brother died
his skin fell off—
a wreath at his feet—
and his bones danced
a jiggy dirge
beside an open grave.

When his brother died
his tears streamed
a cataract of grief
till the casket swam
in a black hole.

When his brother died,
his arteries filled
with shovelfuls of mud
and the valves
of his heart froze.

After his brother died
he nailed shut
windows and doors
and his soul unpacked
in childhood's rooms
memory's rags.

The Wind

The wind knows nothing
about loneliness. Always
it has its arms around something.

Harridan, workhorse, lover,
it screeches, swooshes, sighs,
slamming doors, spinning mill sails,
fingering flesh. It shows itself

in the way it moves
through a foreign body,
billowing skirts, flapping curtains,
angling rain. *In extremis*

it makes missiles of rocks,
cars, billboards, trees.
Roofs lift, towns gasp, heave,
fly apart. At the mercy of forecasts,

we put up shutters, board up
storefronts, follow caravans of fear
away from our lives.

BLUE NUDE

After Pablo Picasso

We do not need to see her face. She has given us her back;
her turned-down head, cradled in her arms, rests upon knees
pressed to her chest as if yearning to return to the womb.

Is she crouched on a bare, cold floor in a vacant room, exiled
to a dream-like nowhere, or awash in the blues of Picasso's
own despondency? We want to know what disengaged her
from the world, hurt her into being an outcast. Did someone die?

Someone like a son or daughter the heart could not live without?
Was she betrayed by a lover? Or shamed by a sin committed
and found out? Perhaps her situation was desperate, bankrupt
of needs and decencies, starved by the indifference of fortune.

Because we will never know, we must look to our own lives.

Despond

When it writes itself
on morning's mirror,
allow it to float like
leaves moving downriver.

It is you. It is still you.

Be with it. Sit with it
as you would sit
silent in a synagogue.

Take it with you,
a pocketbook
whose heavy weight
on your shoulder
bears no complaint.

Keep it close.
Guard it from strangers.

If it wants to cry, let it.
It is the day's weather.
Nothing more.

Take it to bed.
It has stories to tell.

Let it enter your dreams.
Let it talk to your joys,
grievances, sorrows,

the entire family
of who you are.

How to Heal

Begin with the breath.
Let it wash through you
like a zephyr wind.
Open a hole in your body
where your complaints live.
Send a tsunami
to flood their village
and drown their cries.
Let your mind be
as uncluttered as a field
christened in snow.
Go outside.
You have been caged
too long in the airless
room of your illness.
As you move, notice
how the world
has been freshly painted:
red hibiscus aglow
on a green bush; overhead,
an ibis, white wings
dipped in ink; at the base
of the queen palm
the tossed-down coins
of orange seeds.

Housekeeping According to a Yogini

Inhale,
and the household
gods enter,
waving brooms and mops,
carrying buckets
of lemon-scented Joy.

Drunk on letting go,
they exhale
past and future,

confiscate newspapers,
money, mirrors,
sweep and scrub and dust

until the air inside
is so pure
the I that no longer exists
begs to stay forever.

Ode to Small Acts of Kindness

On a morning's walk,
the passing sunlight
of a stranger's smile;
a warm dish
of words for the neighbor
shut off from the world;
loose change
dropped in a canister
for any cause;
in extremity, the squeeze
of a nurse's hand;
Kibbles at the back door
for the abandoned;
for the man stationed
in the crosshairs of traffic,
an extended hand;
remembering
to water houseplants;
purchasing cookies
you'll never eat
from the Girl Scout
outside the grocery store;
any president
inside a holiday card
for the mailman;
in social circumstances,
cell phones silenced
in pocketbooks;
stones on a parent's grave.

On Happiness

A white boat plowing,
the prow lifting and lifting
where two black Labs
lean out, drinking
the rush of wind spray,
the man behind them,
his hair alive as wings,
his lips thrown back,
steering yet relinquishing
himself to something greater
than this bend of river,
his little boat, his two dogs.

LIKE SEA GLASS

The sea has a big mouth.
Like the shark
it will eat anything:
beer bottles, plates,
goblets, windows,
fruit jars, windshields.

Whatever is dropped
into its stomach,
bathed in its juices,
tumbled and ground
to smooth shapes,
over time washes up
as gems on a shoreline.

Like sea glass, so much
that we discard, bury
in a sea of repression,
returns to us, softened
by memory, beautiful
in its forgiveness.

In Defense of Stones

Blameless
against gravity,
blameless
in the hands of fury,
stones would just as soon
stay home
for a long nap.

They are not emotional
like seeds, leaves, the wind.
Yet, palmed
on a sun-glazed walk,
just one
can drive out loneliness.

Comfortable in a crowd,
or a castaway
on beaches, roadsides,
what is more adaptable?

Willingly,
they let the river's tongues
soothe their edges.

Willingly,
they join a community
to keep in, to keep out.

Balanced,
one atop the other,
they show us the way
to stay calm, steady, secure
in the simplicity of being.

III

Huis Clos

After *The Joy of Life* by Paul Delvaux

In the clutch of what could have been
a slow dance, the couple are like boats
moored in the same berth
on a windless day.

Her hand will never leave the blue
mesa of his shoulder, his right arm
will never slip below her waist.

He will never feel her breath
on his neck, inhale her perfume,
or taste the red fruit of her lips.

Their legs will never rub against each other,
igniting a fire, because
it is impossible to dance in a painting.

Though the canvas holds a ballroom,
the world ends at its corners.

This is the torment Sartre warned us about:
Stalled in one place forever, a breath away
from everything you have ever wished for.

Parsing the Heart

The heart has an ear
but not a mouth—
so much left unsaid
in the undressing of doubt.

The heart has its art
of silent deception.
It speaks untruths
by saying nothing.

Don't ask it questions;
the heart hears
what it wants to hear
and answers in Braille.

It defies reason
and knows not itself
why it quickens with touch.

O hungry heart
without a mouth!
O foolish heart
without a brain!
O sweet serenade!

The Difference between Loneliness and Solitude

Loneliness sleepwalks through
an abandoned house. Its bed
is a nest of pillows. Dreaming
of love, it adopts the scraggliest
dog at the shelter and fattens it
on pizza and cookies. The ring
of its doorbell is church bells.

Solitude envies the nautilus
its home built for one. Content
by itself, it lives to make things:
a poem, a painting, a good day...
Hours shrink to seconds when
the Muse visits. If a masterpiece
results, it believes it is a god.

An Introvert's Love Letter to the Rain

All day you have tap-danced
on the roof, written on windows
with wet kisses as now and
again the sky spasmed. I love

how your mood spills into mine,
cautions me to keep tucked inside
myself while streets drown. I love
how you bless me: a mute doorbell,

time without hands, by the sofa
a book I've been meaning to read,
a carafe of chilled chardonnay,
and you (who else, my love,

knows me so well?) content
to be locked outside.

Rumination on Romantic Love

Romance refuses to sleep
its life away in the same bed.

When the storm hushes
and the landscape droops
to a tedious calm,
the heart plots its escape.

So we learn from Shakespeare,
Kierkegaard, Flaubert.

At the death of her affairs,
Madame Bovary chose arsenic—
antidote to a mediocre life.

Ophelia went mad. Juliet died
twice. I slough the past, waking
with windows thrown wide.

Some days in the arms of love,
some days alone.

Embrace of the Drunken Hands

You poured into me as you filled
our wineglasses, emptying the bottle.

Big as you are, when my arms
enclosed you, my fingers kissed
and my body became a country.

I felt your hands on my spine,
the right one descending like syrup,
or a drunk slinking across borders.

In our Argentina, your lips
nursing my breast, your left hand
slipped into the wilderness

inside my jeans. I would have cried
No! but my brain was dreamy. Tell me,

did my hand talk to you through denim
and did you respond? I don't remember

what happened next. We slept,
holding each other, till our hands
sobered up. Then you went home.

How We Happened

You arrived like a letter forwarded to a wrong address,
like a dog's nose to the ground seeking its way home,
like the last peach on a tree, or a stone skipped across
water to land safely in the palm of a leaf. You came

out of a seeming nowhere like a slow-developing sheet
of film; like a fledgling, fanning the air from the lip
of its nest; like the sun, at day's end, content to bleed
into a purpled horizon. Like a bet decided on the flip

of a coin, *Heads,* you called. And I answered, the way
mourning doves volley songs through a stand of pines,
a bounced ball returns to a child's hand, or a stray
shadows a boy's heart to a door. Like a trumpet vine

to a hummingbird, I invited you in. *Stay!* I said,
Stay like a rock washed smooth by a river. And you did.

Being with You

is like exploring byways
of a country no cartographer
ever managed to map.
Ice-slicked even in summer,
roads climb and dip
with a roller coaster's grade.
Vertiginous curves
let out on straightaways
edged in blood-red poppies.
There are no speed limits
or rest stops. One way
and dead end streets
do not exist.
Traffic lights
are always green.

Being without You

is like swimming laps
in a bathtub or drowning
in a puddle of rain.
Love needs a conjunction,
x *and* y. One alone
is a rump grounded
on a seesaw, a flag
on a windless day.
What use the syrup
of my voice,
the gentle fingers
of my words?
What use
these puckered lips,
this cupped torso
nights alone?

Questions before Moving In Together

Years ago, after my divorce,
I packed up aprons, culinary books.

Darling, do you like to cook?

Now that chores are unassigned,
would you do the laundry, sweep
and dust while I recline?

*To save time, let's assume
the walk-in closet is mine.*

In the confines of shared rooms,
would there be a place
for all my moods? And, honey,

would it be rude
to ask for daily solitude?

Don't you agree a modicum
of privacy should be preserved?

Separate bathrooms are de rigueur.

If I retire before you, dear,
would you sulk?

Please don't clone me to your clock.

When we're in bed,
would you get upset
if my cat
snoozles on my chest?

Quite frankly, there's nothing
you can do about that.

If my questions unsettle you,
sweetheart we would best

keep together by living apart.

THE RING

I found it on the internet, a handmade
beauty, white gold and yellow gold—
the moon and sun sculpted to hold
one perfect diamond. I was afraid
he'd scoff at my presumption, our years
imperfect, disparity trumped by desire.
But time has a leaking heart; the fire
soon goes out. He had shared his fears,

founded in history, a square dance
of changing partners. I showed the ring.
He smiled, an awful smile, startling
me. Oh, if I'd only left luck to chance!
Now what I want more than anything
is not to be engaged by circumstance.

The Wedding

After *La Mariée* by Marc Chagall

Suspended between earth and sky,
between the real and the imagined,
a young bride floats, shamelessly dressed
in a red gown, framed by a white veil as if
her vows have lifted her out of darkness.

Suspended between earth and sky,
between the real and the imagined,
her mate hovers, one hand on her shoulder,
the other clutching her head as if he would
keep her and this moment fixed forever.

Suspended between earth and sky,
between the real and the imagined,
a man with a goat's head sweeps his bow,
his violoncello's blue notes falling on the
village below where ordinary life waits.

IV

SOLOIST

Like an ornament
at the apex of a clay roof
a single bird will perch,
lord of the highest view.

This morning it's a dove
dissolving against the soft
grey of an overcast sky.
Better than high branches

or high wires, here he is
a soloist, rooster of the skies,
loosening his six-note aria
on the empty street below.

From my open window
in an adjacent building,
I sit watching, listening
to his abandoned heart,

thinking, this is the way
a poem writes itself,
note by solitary note
on the prevailing air.

A Brief Encounter

A rustling shivers
through high branches.
Climbing, sailing, leaping,
one squirrel launches

a trajectory of waking,
life pouring into life,
its breadth and length,
sparing not one leaf.

Watching him, now
watching me, he peeks
from sunlit openings,
circling as I speak

in dulcet clicks, a greeting.
Such a tease, his head
disappearing,
reappearing

as if what is said
is another branch
beneath his spry feet.
In the language of tails,

in a tale's leitmotif,
from a low branch
he answers
scribbling the air.

CROW

Atop a lamppost,
against a dusky sky—
a silhouette
cut in tar paper.

Years ago
someone
whose reasoning
I failed to decipher
gave her to me—
my sobriquet. Crow,

the keenest of birds,
never stirred
a feather
of her priestly robe
while I strained my neck.

When she spoke,
short, rough syllables
clearing her throat,

a threnody
composed
of a singular note,

she needed no one
to listen
or sound back.

For the Love of Certain Spaces

The moon's watermark
on a brightening sky,
highways that fall away
to the horizon, a dirt trail
beneath arched trees,
avenues lined in the airy
giants of Australian pines,
woodlands glazed in ice,
a roadside intoxicated
with poppies, wetlands
crowned with duckweed
and the yellow fists
of spatterdock, islands
tremulous with wings,
a shoreline's give and take
over which a pelican
pulls a string of pelicans,
the fifty blues of the ocean,
a solitary cabin beside
a silvery stream,
the black snake
of a mountain pass,
a cave's musky breath,
dusk's descending veils,
on an evening flight
from 3,000 feet
the fallen constellations
of city lights, pressing
down in the pure dark
of the countryside
the brilliant stars.

Recalling the Blue Ridge in Summer

Sunlit, a thousand tinctures of green.
Up, up through fretwork, a sparrow's
clanky phrases, a cardinal's flames.
Rustling a tulip poplar's leaves,
the question marks of a squirrel's tail.
Through shrubby interstices, the white
flags of skittish deer. Along dirt trails,
hieroglyphic prints and steamy scat
of red fox, black bear. Rinsing the air,
the tiny mouths of violets. As if a name
could tame what's wild, black-eyed
Susan, bouncing bet, butter-and-eggs,
Queen Anne's lace. Deep in shadow
where roots snake, like items dropped
in a fairytale, lady's slippers, Indian pipes.

Autumn at Chesley Creek Farm

Morning by the creek
where red and yellow leaves float,
I startled a doe.

Beneath a blazed tree,
a patch of Indian pipes
hid from the noon sun.

On the porch at dusk,
I sipped a glass of claret
wrapped in a wool shawl.

At night while I slept,
a white river of moonlight
streamed into my dreams.

EDEN COTTAGE

Charlottesville, VA

Over clay and blue stone
the creek's song keeps going
thin in its dry throat.

The morning-wet grass
is seeded with sound,
a muted unwinding of gears.

Green backed with green
deepens in shadow.
Wind rustle. Bird chatter.

Now sound transmutes
into motion, as if song,
internalized, fuels the wings.

A goldfinch lasers
a trajectory, hickory to feeder.
The air hums like a taut wire.

Beyond, July's uncut fields
dance to a reel that skirts
the registers of the human ear.

Morikami Gardens

Red azaleas blazed the trail
that wound around a lake
past gardens of raked pebbles,
trickling waterfalls, a forest
of yellow and green
bamboo the breeze clacked.

Wooden benches along the edge
invited me to rest and view
a stream of orange-splashed koi,
the clustered water lilies so like
Monet's paintings in Giverny.

Past the giant Buddha, serene
in reclining layers of stone flesh,
I came to a memorial garden
where skippers and swallowtails
fluttered above lavender phlox.

Their nervous wings landed
and lifted quickly as if pleasure
could only be granted in tiny sips.

THE VISIT

The house, ordinary,
wood-sided, a tin roof,
but from the back porch,
stretching for miles
a river, sun-sparkling,
nights, the floating stars...

Opposite, fields of wheat
wind-danced, brushed
by red and yellow epaulets
flapping, flitting, calling
conk-la-ree!...

Meandering roads edged
in goldenrod, foxglove,
larkspur, hawkweed,
my eyes climbing trees,
trees climbing mountains...

Drunk on clean air,
how could I leave a place
that said to me, *Stay!*

But I was only a visitor,
as I am in all my dreams.

FROM *THE MANUAL FOR SOUTH FLORIDA TOURISM*

Look up
through the tracery
of twigs and leaves
to the flaming crown
of the poinciana,
and breathe.

Watch
herons and anhingas
skim across duckweed
where hyacinths
and the purple
gallinule live,
and breathe.

Feel
the sun
filter through fronds
while the hours
loaf in a hammock,
and breathe.

Listen
to the gulls'
high-pitched squeals
chase the fishing boat's
wake to shore,
and breathe.

Follow
the pitchfork
prints of terns
on a foam-lapped
edge where
blue meets blue,
and breathe.

Taste
the salty breeze
that thins near
the sea grape hedge
to fumes and the prattle

of billboards
before you leave,
and breathe.

THE CRACKED POT, A RETELLING

Each day the old woman
filled two pots
with cool stream water.

Their weight at either end of a stick,
hard across her neck,
balanced her stride,

but as she walked her right shoulder
dipped, the other
tilted toward the sky,

leaving a trail
for the hungry earth.
When she arrived home,

the perfect pot was full, the other,
only half full. *Fool!*
the villagers cried, *Cracked!*

to carry a leaky pot
the long walk home
under the hot eye of the sun.

One day the cracked pot fell
sullen and spoke to its bearer:
I am full of shame,

cutting your efforts in half.
Your hard work deserves better.
The old woman only smiled.

In spring, as she walked
to the stream, the left side
of the trail

had come into blossom:
Jewels of Opar, rain lily,
golden iris.

The Backyard

Norfolk, Virginia

I don't miss the house. I don't miss the doorbell
and mail slot, the sound of the driveway scattering stones.
From my study two stories up, from the lawn chair
that eased my afternoons, I would wait for the Muse
to arrive on the Lafayette River.

She loved disguises: the egret's mid-river meditation;
the Canada goose, faithful to the lip of land where
his mate nested; in the pines, the doves' volleyed lament;
drunk on mulberries, June birds splatting against glass.

Even things without wings had wings: the dance
of the feeder; April's rain of cherry blossoms; a red bud,
planted in memory of my daughter; squirrels leaping like
laughter osier to osier; angel wings in the forgiving snow.

When winds whipped Tidewater, she rode the black
river's fury to my back door. O merciful! And stopped.

The Mating

In the expectant stillness
of dance partners
they face each other
tuned to an
inner music
that sets their heads
pumping, pumping,
his tail shaking
like a happy dog's
till in one precise
movement
he mounts,
pounces really,
his gleaming body
in full vibrato,
then, in a blink
he's off
circling her,
his wake
like an echo
widening out
from the cove's heart.

TURKEY BUZZARDS

Wings uplifted in a V
they soar in wobbly circles,
riding thermals
to scan the countryside,

or steered by smell
they glide low,
their shadows gracing
pastures, dumpsters,
the black tablecloths
of highways.

A fresh kill
will draw a wake,
bald heads bobbing,
hooked bills tearing
into any sick
or breathless thing.

At night they retreat
to the skeletons
of hollow trees,
their only song a dirge
of grunts and hisses.

Roseate Spoonbill

Would that I had the efficient scoop
to fill a bucket like a pelican

or the egret's bill to stab hunger
and toss it down the long chute

of my gullet. In mangroves,
I lower the flattened spoon

of my beak, sifting muddy water
for the wriggle of small fish,

my head swinging side to side
as if I were saying *No!*

to my reflected image. Once,
I was valued for my beauty

and beauty was the death of me.
My scarlet plumes fanned faces,

nested on ladies' heads.
No longer fashionable,

now I fear sprawling malls
and burgeoning developments

that stole the rookery
where once my mate waited

for my love dance,
my clapping mandibles.

V

Still Life in Blue

After *Difficult Child* by Lisa Hess Hesselgrave

Nothing is happening in the world of her room.
The ivories lie still as teeth in a jar. Yesterday
she played a lively toccata, her hands dancing
the keys. Today she sits, hands in lap like a child
waiting to be told when to lift the fork and eat.

The table is bare, her shadow staining its white cloth.
Is she waiting for something, a ring, a knock, to break
the spell that keeps her frozen in the hard-back chair?
Perhaps she has disappeared into prayer, her thoughts
impervious to time as an hourglass drained of sand.

Maybe this is what death would feel like—
a featureless globe atop a mute piano,
a strapless gown for shroud, and you, forever
going nowhere in the coffin of a blue room.

A Brief History

When I was a girl
I wished for breasts.
I wanted lips
old enough
for Cotton-Candy-
Pink lipstick, for legs
a second skin
of silk, feet tipped
in the sinful slide
of 3-inch heels. Nights
I dreamed
a prince's kiss
would boot me
into living.

A young woman,
I flashed my hips
like whirligigs,
used bait:
a honeyed smile,
fishnet, leather,
black lace.
Lickety-split,
I caught a husband,
a house, two children,
pots and pans,
shopping lists,
calendars washed
in a sea of ink.

After the divorce, after
a string of lovers, after
the children left, after
Prozac, after
an analyst, after
I no longer
needed the mirrors
of men's eyes
or my name
in headlines, after
I gave away
designer labels
for gravity's
housedress,

I found myself—
a woman
alone
on a mountain top
dancing naked
beneath the tipped
smile of a moon
and the winking stars.

To All the Men I Have Loved

No, I won't give a number
or reveal names.
Matters of intimacy
are best kept
under covers.

I could divide you
into categories:
greatest lovers,
most thoughtful,
neediest, artists,
business suits,
bad boys, *mensches,*
or in years
by staying power.

To be just,
I refuse
to simplify the heart's
complexity
to one dimension.

I remember the heat
of lovemaking,
the relentless clock
that put the fire out,
the slammed door
of arguments
that fueled bliss,

jouissance
that outlasted
the moon and stars,

so many faces
blurred, coalesced
by memory,
it's as if
now
we all sleep
together
in the same bed.

Now That I Am Old

I am no longer afraid
of shadows,
snapping teeth,
the clap and slash
of split skies,
prayers unanswered
for the soul's keep.

I am no longer afraid
of being loved
or not being loved.

I am no longer afraid
of what has no face:
pestilence, floods,
nuclear bombs.

No one escapes
the indifferent flame,
earth's hunger.

Open the gates
of the asylum, the prison.
I will take my chances.

But you,
innocent one,
who sits smiling
at the beating
of sorrow's dog,
of you I am afraid.

ARGUMENTS AGAINST A HEARING AID

I have no difficulty carrying on conversations
with myself. In dreams my hearing's perfect.

There's more room for silence—that stilled pond
upon which my best thoughts float.

Never one for idle talk, I get by with a head shake
and a smile. Eventually eyes, those quick learners,

pick up a second language. As for the world,
despair is a bottom feeder, it cups its ear

to bad news. Every day I reduce the number
of war dead, starving children, natural disasters.

I keep telling myself, you'll never miss
the dance of squirrels mornings on the tin roof;

behind the house, the kiss of the kingfisher
puncturing a hole in the Lafayette River;

the plucked heart of a Brahms concerto;
the vespers of birdsong in the pines.

Face It

I've been your calling card,
the mask you wear
in public rooms,

the one who has had
a hard time
staying friends

with mirrors.
Each morning
you stare above the sink

as you wash sleep off,
afraid of the stranger
you're becoming.

Practice loving lines
that bracket your mouth
as if they were

merely time's aside
resting now
in the parentheses

of a frown.
What of the empty purses
beneath your eyes,

the hound-dog
jowls that shake
with laughter?

For heaven's sake,
be generous. Be kind.
Let wrinkles write

you're wise. Read me
as the bountiful
course your life has taken.

Good Intentions

Pear trees burst into blossom.
Sun sparkles off the blue Fiesta
he no longer drives. His neighbor

is out walking his dog. Stop. Start.
Stop. A dog believes he owns
his street and must sniff

before signing the right spot.
The man has grown used to living
alone. Everything he touches—

doorknobs, banister, a spoon—
had been touched years ago
by his wife and children. And yet

he feels the loss, the days keep
falling into a black river.
He is careful not to mention this.

Yesterday, his two sons brought
picturesque brochures, good
intentions. He can still bake

a chicken on Sunday and make
it last the week. He remembers
his pills. The April air is redolent.

After breakfast, he will work
in the garden, clear weeds
from the emerging daffodils.

How to Stage Regret

Hire your heart to edit your history
and overwrite the ego's scripts.
Remove all mirrors from the set,
those culprits of self-interest.

Let Mother Teresa direct
(Who better to coach your actions!)
so that the casts' unspoken
needs guide your performance.

To circumvent stardom's pitfalls,
think of yourself as embodying
a cameo role. Let third-person
pronouns play the protagonists

as you wait in the wings for the chance
to support, praise, comfort, assist.
Avoid the temptation of finding
your person perfect, an exemplar

of compassion that would turn
selflessness into arrogance. Introduce
a Greek chorus in each act to express,
in wailing interludes, the apologies

you should have made. For audience,
the living and the dead: mother, father,
daughter, lover, friend—so that
at curtain's fall you may be forgiven.

Winter's Lessons

Trees stripped of summer's store
and fall's giveaway reveal the bones
of what stays. The river frozen

to the shore's lip speaks less,
keeps to itself what belongs to itself.
The bear in his den, the bat suspended

in his cave, know when to sleep
and when to wake. No longer
hitched to the world's rhythms,

no longer ruled by appetite, they wait
for an inner pull to rouse them.
And what is more instructional

than snowfall, its knack for making
the familiar new. Or night, arriving early,
flooding its borders at both ends.

COMMUTERS

For this brief ride,
this bridge between
clocked time,
they place their cares
in the passenger seat.

Soon they will enter
well-lit rooms where
stocks rise or dip
and bombs burst
in foreign cities.

If there is a family,
a dinner waiting,
this, too, will need
work.

For now, the sun
sputtering on the horizon,
their lives set
on cruise control,
they lean into the dark.

Her Nightmare

She is driving. She isn't driving.
The car slips into a tunnel.
Not death's tunnel, no flickering
light at the end, no white funnel

shooting into heaven
clutched in Christ's arms.
In the pitch darkness, the walls
compress, like the room

in Poe's story, metal shrinking
around the condemned;
his body seared and writhing,
pushed to the edge.

But in her nightmare, screams
evoke no trumpets; walls
fail to fall back. She isn't driving.
She is driving down a hall

thick with mist, wrapped
in the cloud of her last breath,
atom by atom disintegrating
the way fire loves itself to death.

ANGELICA AND THE HERMIT

After Peter Paul Rubens

O Angelica, your creamy flesh posed
like an oversize calendar girl, arms
thrown back, torso torqued to expose
the copious banquet of your charms

offered up on a vermilion platter,
surely this is the manifestation
of your own desire. In your dream,
whose gaze awakens sensation

in every pore? Whose hands explore
the landscape, fold upon fold,
of your voluptuousness? Certainly
not the predatory claws of an old

man. Sleep, Angelica, forevermore
sleep in the sweet arms of your
dream, safe from the nightmare
that waits at waking's door.

Bedtime Imperative

Turn off the TV.
Turn off the lights.

Open the windows.
Open your hinged heart.

Let night enter,
black-faced, spilling
moonlight across the floor.

Turn down the covers.

Turn down the voice
of the caviller in your head.

Let go of lists.
Let go of your age.

Rejoice in the gift
of cool sheets.

Rejoice in the respite
of an unmanned skiff
adrift on a lake
strewn with stars.

Close your eyes.

Let curtains fall.
Let curtains rise.

Bella Donna

After *Resting Somnambulist IV* by Pyke Koch

Let the candle go out.
Put the sewing machine to bed.
Do not worry. When you wake

sunlight will stitch the world back
to a motley quilt. Relax

as your mattress greens
with nightshade's leaves.

Feel yourself fall
into a delirium
beneath a chuppah of stars.

Bella Donna, here in this dream,
on this plain of death,
know you are truly alive.

Last Wishes

As I contrived a life
out of the box,
scatter my death
on the wind's back.

Let me live again
to mine the earth
in the belly of a worm.

For dirge, rain
on a tin roof,
a dog's yelp,
the laughter of leaves.

No makeup,
no touched-up
script for eulogy.

Say I was happily flawed.
Say I was human.

Acknowledgments

I am grateful to the editors of the journals in which these poems, several in different form, first appeared.

Angle—Journal of Poetry in English: "Rousseau's Last Painting," "*Angelica and the Hermit*"
Avatar Review: "Now That I Am Old," "Still Life in Blue"
Cardinal Sins Journal: "The Mandate"
Damselfly Press: "Roseate Spoonbill"
Harbinger Asylum: "David, O David," "The Difference between Loneliness and Solitude"
Innisfree Poetry Journal: "In Defense of Stones," "What She Longed For," "Winter's Lessons"
Iodine Poetry Journal: "The Seafarer's Wife," "The Backyard"
Ithaca Lit: "The Politics of Fingers"
Lighthouse Point Magazine: "From *The Manual for South Florida Tourism*"
Liquid Imagination: "When His Brother Died"
Minerva Rising: "A Brief History," "Adrift," "Bella Donna"
Off the Coast: "The Ring," "An Introvert's Love Letter to the Rain," "Day's End"
Passager: "Arguments against a Hearing Aid"
Piedmont Journal of Poetry & Fiction: "Autumn at Chesley Creek Farm," "Eden Cottage," "Recalling the Blue Ridge in Summer," "Turkey Buzzards"
Poetry Quarterly: "Freight of Moods"
Poetry Super Highway: "How to Ripen," "One Apple"
Saw Palm Florida Literature and Art: "Morikami Gardens
Silver Blade: "For the Love of Certain Spaces," "How We Happened"
S/tick: "Her Nightmare"

Stoneboat: "Two Crows"
Sunset Liminal: "Face It," "Good Intentions," "To All the Men I
    Have Loved"
The Aurorean: "Ars Poetica"

"Daphne's Plea" was the July 2013 winner of the Goodreads
Poetry Contest and appeared in its newsletter.

"Last Wishes" was featured in John Siegfried's "Writing My Own
Obituary" (*Letters,* March 8, 2013).

A number of these poems appeared in the author's chapbook
Cracks (FutureCycle Press, 2015).

I am grateful to Mary-Jean Kledzik and Mary McCue for their
critical feedback on this manuscript, and to Jon Frangipane,
Wendell Abern, and the other members of the Fort Lauderdale
Writers' Group for their invaluable support. Kudos to Diane
Kistner, my incomparable editor, for her belief in my work and
production of a flawless book.

*Cover artwork, "The Dream" by Henri Rousseau; author photo
by Susan Calace-Wilklow; cover and interior book design by Diane
Kistner from the author's concept; Adobe Garamond Pro text and
Foglihten titling.*

About FutureCycle Press

FutureCycle Press is dedicated to publishing lasting English-language poetry books, chapbooks, and anthologies in both print-on-demand and Kindle ebook formats. Founded in 2007 by long-time independent editor/publishers and partners Diane Kistner and Robert S. King, the press incorporated as a nonprofit in 2012. A number of our editors are distinguished poets and writers in their own right, and we have been actively involved in the small press movement going back to the early seventies.

The FutureCycle Poetry Book Prize and honorarium is awarded annually for the best full-length volume of poetry we publish in a calendar year. Introduced in 2013, our Good Works projects are anthologies devoted to issues of universal significance, with all proceeds donated to a related worthy cause. Our Selected Poems series highlights contemporary poets with a substantial body of work to their credit; with this series we strive to resurrect work that has had limited distribution and is now out of print.

We are dedicated to giving all of the authors we publish the care their work deserves, making our catalog of titles the most diverse and distinguished it can be, and paying forward any earnings to fund more great books.

We've learned a few things about independent publishing over the years. We've also evolved a unique, resilient publishing model that allows us to focus mainly on vetting and preserving for posterity poetry collections of exceptional quality without becoming overwhelmed with bookkeeping and mailing, fundraising activities, or taxing editorial and production "bubbles." To find out more about what we are doing, visit www.futurecycle.org.

THE FUTURECYCLE POETRY BOOK PRIZE

All full-length volumes of poetry published by FutureCycle Press in a given calendar year are considered for the annual FutureCycle Poetry Book Prize. This allows us to consider each submission on its own merits, outside of the context of a contest. Too, the judges see the finished book, which will have benefitted from the beautiful book design and strong editorial gloss we are famous for.

The book ranked the best in judging is announced as the prize-winner in the subsequent year. There is no fixed monetary award; instead, the winning poet receives an honorarium of 20% of the total net royalties from all poetry books and chapbooks the press sold online in the year the winning book was published. The winner is also accorded the honor of being on the panel of judges for the next year's competition; all judges receive copies of all contending books to keep for their personal library.

68034766R00061

Made in the USA
Charleston, SC
03 March 2017